Another Way of Loving Death

Another Way of Loving Death

poems
by Jeremy Ra

~ 2023 ~

Another Way of Loving Death
© Copyright 2023 Jeremy Ra
All rights reserved. No part of this book may be used or reproduced in any manner whatsoever without written permission from either the author or the publisher, except in the case of credited epigraphs or brief quotations embedded in articles or reviews.

Editor-in-chief
Eric Morago

Editor Emeritus
Michael Miller

Marketing Specialist
Ellen Webre

Proofreader
LeAnne Hunt

Front cover art
Mei Xian Qui

Author photo
Alexis Rhone Fancher

Book design
Michael Wada

Moon Tide logo design
Abraham Gomez

Another Way of Loving Death is published by Moon Tide Press

Moon Tide Press
6709 Washington Ave. #9297
Whittier, CA 90608
www.moontidepress.com

FIRST EDITION

Printed in the United States of America

ISBN #978-1-957799-07-0

Contents

Foreword by Aruni Wijesinghe	*6*
To the Boy Who Wanted Flames as Hair	11
Humanity	13
Dumplings (Jiaozi)	14
Slot Machine	15
The Audition	17
Burning in Winter	18
Boys Sleeping	19
Foolish Dreams Are All I Know	21
Last Time I Saw Eve	22
The Legend of a Swordswoman	23
Expired LA Times Subscription	26
Do Not Ask Why	27
Archeology of a Phone Call	28
What Jesus Said While in Line for the Bathroom	30
Firstborn	31
Humming and Shaving	32
A Hole in the Sky	33
You Will Be Done	34
My Father's Mother That My Mother Hated	35
In the Thick Night, We Kiss the Flame	38
About the Author	*40*
Acknowledgements	*41*

Foreword

We each view new stories through individual cultural lenses. With good poetry, we find new stars to incorporate into our internal galaxies. But with the best poems, we recognize familiar constellations revolving in our night skies. Such is the case with reading the poems contained in *Another Way of Loving Death,* Jeremy Ra's debut collection.

As soon as I opened this collection I was immersed in the poet's rich imagination, a wilderness where ancestral myth and modern-day happenstance comingle. Ra's subjects range from immigrant sensibilities to family mythology, the complexity of parent-child relationships, his own queer identity, and expanded concepts of mortality and faith. Ultimately, Ra's journeys take us deep into the human heart and the aching for intimacy that haunts us all.

Ra's narrative traverses an endlessly shifting geographic map, moving from Hawaii to Korea to Las Vegas and back to his current home in Los Angeles. He deftly leads the reader through a migratory life in which he honors his Asian heritage while turning a critical eye on family tradition. In so doing, he creates a mythology were the speaker is cast in the roles of saint, sinner and congregant simultaneously. Whether making dumplings en famille or chasing mute ghosts longing for conversation, the poet examines the intricacies of immigrant families without pretense or sentiment. Disarmingly, he invites the reader to draw up a chair and share in both the family meal and the family drama.

The poet fearlessly tackles the big questions of impermanence and human frailty with both pathos and humor. At one turn he lets himself quietly out of the life of an ex-lover; in a different scene, he shepherds dying family members through loss and estrangement, acknowledging that some connections are necessarily missed. These partings are sketched sometimes with irony, often with unflinching candor, but always with compassion. His religious faith maintains a certain wide-eyed innocence, even in the gritty light of mornings after.

Ra honors every facet of his complex identity in his work. Ultimately, his collection explores what it means to be quintessentially American. This ability of the poet to inhabit multiple universes moved me the most. The sense of recognition compelled me to examine what it means be a bridge between cultures, traditions, orientations and schools of thought. He references Chinese mythology while surviving long nights in Los Angeles. One night, an ancestral patriarch scales his apartment building; another night, the poet shares the dawn's last cigarette with total strangers. The search for human connection is a poignant thread throughout Ra's work, whether at a dying grandmother's bedside or on the walk to and from school with uniformed school crushes. The poet is part chameleon and part chimera as he opens windows into both his own psyche and the realities of anyone who has walked the tightrope that connects different worlds.

    I was blessed to meet Jeremy Ra in a poetry workshop several years ago and, based on our common subjects and points of view, I knew we would be fast friends. It has been thrilling to witness the inception, development, and final realization of this stunning debut collection. I am privileged to write in support of this project.

— Aruni Wijesinghe, author of *2 Revere Place* and *The Litany of Missing*

For, where eros is lack, its activation calls for three structural components—lovers, beloved, and that which comes between them.

— Anne Carson, *Eros, the Bittersweet*

To Bette Davis, Gena Rowlands, Romy Schneider... To all actresses who have played actresses, to all women who act, to all men who act and become women, to all the people who want to be mothers. To my mother.

— Pedro Almodóvar, Dedication, *Todo Sobre Mi Madre*

To the Boy Who Wanted Flames as Hair

Don't trust a man who says *trust me*.

Question everything.

Remember what Erykah Badu said: *what good do your words do when they can't understand you?*

Searching for the right words will feel like fishing without a hook.

It's important to know that you were once happy, even if it's not true.

You'll never stop mourning your pets. Get over it. Or not.

Stop making men you like listen to "Rid of Me"—no romance ever started with you yelling *I'm gonna make you lick my injuries till you say don't you wish you never, never met her.*

The luminous things you can't share light a corner in you that others can't corrupt.

What you need isn't more clothes—you need a tailor.

You'll make friends who will teach you love, and as a result, you'll lose some of them.

Write essays about persona poems.

Write persona poems.

Be careful what you accept about yourself, and others.

You'll learn that "safe word" was invented because saying "no" wasn't enough.

You will tell so many lies, but you'll never get good at it.

Once, twice you will ask yourself if everything will be solved if you just jumped off this bridge.

The answer is no.

I need you to trust me.

Humanity

The church gave her a choir because she sang like bird and looked like bird and Brenda was a bird. She owed us so many poems.

— Bot Obituary for Brenda Tent

I went out one night, my whole being dizzy.
How the ground pulled me down.
I copied a love that wasn't mine,
didn't know how to get home.
The fraught night trembled in my voice.

I had a bottle of good wine—really good wine—
half-drunk, but I couldn't drink anymore.
How I tried to give it away to a man in a tent
with sparkles in his eyes, and he told me
he was allergic to yeast.

I was in Vegas once, twice, seventy times—
and I met a man who belonged
to a friend, and when we walked back
from the bathroom—how he held my hand,
so I could forget my feminism for a bit.

Notice how my stanzas start with "I"—
I am tired of traumas too, the quicksand
that is me. I love you, humanity,
even your cruelty. Brenda, you are a bird now.

Fly—I'll pay your debt.

Dumplings (*Jiaozi*)

Jiaozi were originally referred to as "tender ears" (Chinese:嬌耳; pinyin: *jiao'er*) because they were used to treat frostbitten ears.

[Textual interpretation: the tender ears of the son of horns]

On a frosty morning, the family separates the dough
into small wrappers, fills them with a pinched ball
of pork rolled with scallions, sauce, and chives.
With water, we seal the dough into half-moons
over and over till the swelling dumplings fill the counter.
It is not money that makes a family rich. The gods
have settled into the kitchen, and we have been crowded
ever since. I can never grab the pinch
quite right, so the half-moons don't keep their pregnancy
in the boiling water. My grandmother always eats
the half-moons I ruined first. She alone is left
to remember the journey the family made
on a boat to reach Seoul from Shan Dong—
dumplings the only heirloom she could carry.
With an air of constant mourning for a son,
my uncle says she is quiet and has no favorites,
so any story we tell can never be untrue.
With each chatter thrown into the dinner pyre,
she buries a lot more than a son, over and over.
The chives are potent but not enough to ward off
the dead, our relatives who dance with the steam
in the distance. We know the shapes
of laughter and mime them.

* * *

My grandmother hangs
with the chived ghosts in the air—
she stares at me with a self-devouring gaze,
divided from me by several oceans. She holds
my hands that unwrap the half-moons—
fills my ears with dumplings.

Slot Machine

I got tired of competing with dead people
for attention; I can't seem to die
or accomplish at the pace they do.

So, I sit in front of the slot machine,
zombified, as mother points out.
She didn't like her in-laws

who made her pay for every meal
when she had abandoned her blood
to be at Honolulu beach,

selling oceanic trinkets to tourists.
A false crest had won her,
a house that always reunited in Vegas.

How was she supposed to know
that the house always wins,
sitting in front of the penny slots

pushing the sticky buttons
that turned the screen smudged gray
with all-night fuckery of edging

about hopes and inarticulate
dreams? The big number above the screen
crept up like a stock ticker.

And surely, didn't she deserve it—

among dirty quarter trickles
and having to eat at the buffets long enough
for two meals each night

while her husband was god-
knows-where. Surely, once, the creaky spin
of the slots had aroused her.

She walked in search of that perfect
lever that would serenade her
in the tune of looted gold.

She stayed up all night
with the ladies of the casino,
a part of her still sad

when the bells didn't choose her
despite her good sense.

The slots kept turning,
and after paying a hundred dollars
for three drinks, the secret to winning
seemed to lie in appearances.

Mother, I loved a married man
despite knowing the house always wins.

The Audition

I escape judgments
at your loft, a renovated building
in the Arts District, and stumble
onto a stage you prepared
with impossibly high ceilings,
like notes from an aria
I can't hit. The imposing wine-red
curtains, you say,
had to be custom-fitted, sway.
The bathroom sections off
thin familiarity with frosted glass.
The open space seems intent
on forcing my cards.
In your connoisseur hands,
I am the finest wine
south of Napa—
uncorked of discomfort, I undress.

When I lose my way after a party
you didn't want to attend,
a truck totals my car.
You scoop me up
in your Mercedes, and I crawl out
of my shellshock during dinner
coaxed by our reflection
at Bäco Mercat. I imbibe the ease
at a frequency I cannot afford.
I mingle with the spouses
whose verbs are polished
to a presentable sheen.

I sleep over that night.
But, restless before dawn,
I put on the black suit
I got from an outlet,
go out the door holding my shoes.
You wake for a second—
ask me if I need a ride,
and I lie,
but not in the way you want.

Burning in Winter

We bought a Christmas tree, but then
gathered at my aunt's house
where the pagoda's once verdant roof
peeled and rattled under the gait of the cats
who paced like guardians of a tomb.

Every winter, the neighbors left a sacrifice
of birth-blind kittens in a plastic bag—
so often that, at Christmas, they became the gift
I expected when I got to the house. My aunt's dog
that raised the surviving kittens came slobbering

like it didn't know how to stop living
in the same house where incense burned
before a portrait of a woman who wouldn't
stop dying. I never questioned the heat
from the hot pot, nor what I saw in the subway ads

of families in red hats cooking on electric grills.
Santa and every amen haunted our Christmas tree
by the doorway, a present underneath left unopened,
as my parents took me back to our cold apartment
in clothes that smelt of fish and ash.

Boys Sleeping

Running into you in the school bathroom
underlines me like a book title.
I synopsize excuses you'd make

to stand closer. We walk home seemingly
together, stumble into booths
where we spend more than our allowances

on sticker pictures that we paste
to the back of our hidden diaries
with Sanrio stationery. I see my veins glow

in a way they shouldn't. We don't slip
notes to each other in classes, but somehow
find a way to walk home together, blended

with other boys in the same uniforms.
At our friend's house, whose parents
are away, we watch a porno. I wonder

if anyone notices our gazes
are elsewhere. Our story isn't here, even
in the disrobing of the primal.

Maybe we were created on the 8th day
because god installed cable TV
when he got tired of watching

the same old sex. Do you remember,
too, that once, flesh was mere wound,
the layer beneath the skin housing

a map of vessels? We invent a science
project we must work on that lets me
sleepover on a twin bed,

lights out, a quilt patterned
with little robots, your body heaves
next to mine—a running river, glistening,

noisy from the amphibians flailing
within. O rising croaks,
abduct us from the well we can't climb—

the world won't hear us, but the night
remembers this breath that shrouded
boys with the bluest veins.

Foolish Dreams Are All I Know

Elon Musk has sent satellites into the sky that look like stars. We may be the last generation to gaze into the true night sky.

— Steven Soderbergh, *Let Them All Talk*

I thought I saw a comet crash
into the front of my balcony
as the car alarm a motorcycle
set off had just been lulled.

Yet there he was, drunk-shamed,
bewildered as a newborn,
and wings scorched from his flight—
my neighbor who lived 3 stories up.

I sort of knew his troubles:
he had lost his girlfriend, his job, his grip
on the rails of his patio—a man, fallen
with red-well eyes.

Vodka led his plunge but prevented
permanent fracture, and he thieved
out one night from under my care—
will send forwarding address when I have it.

These days, even the stars aren't
honest, satellites mock our signs.
Folly keeps these dark nights at bay—
gives wings back to an Icarus.

Last Time I Saw Eve[1]

When I opened the laundry-room door,
smoke trundled out—
my mom emerged from behind the gauzy
thickness, for a moment indomitable
as Bette Davis presiding god-like
over all her silver-screen aches.
As the smoke faded,
she said dad must have lit one
before he left for work.
Even then I knew my dad
who smoked in public
would not have gone through the trouble
to hide in the laundry room
for a single cigarette,
that such layers of smoke
couldn't have been cast
in vocational habit, no—
such thick exhales
were fabricated with thought,
cocooning her from the paring
knife, the cleaving knife, the carve
of the bone still brewing in the pot,
always noises in the pot.
I wanted nothing
but to learn her solitude
when I stole her cigarettes,
studying the lipstick around
the snuffed butts, as if she kissed
death back and left the smear
of her birthright like crime-
scene evidence.
And I knew in the regret
of tasting that regret,
how she plunged a curtain
around her to burn the things
she couldn't say.

---

[1] Inspired by Cathy Colman's poems in *Time Crunch*.

The Legend of a Swordswoman

I.

I was about six
the first time I saw her kill a man.
No, not this, I thought—

berating a subway ticket agent
who shooed away her complaints,
Piece of expired shit who forgot to die.

I see his death-wish float up like incense.
Poor fellow.
What price must he pay

for a flick of the wrist?
Men like him have tried
for women to leave without a fuss.

In hell, no doubt he will think,
Well, that wasn't enough sin.
You don't understand,

you men, you silly men—
did you not see how she shreds
the centuries of my father's tall heritage

at a family banquet?
The chattering of who owned what land
and how much money; then her:

*How come you have nothing now
that even a meal becomes a debt?*
Watching the myths fall around me,

mother slowly becomes a prayer
that I whisper when I must fight
against the ones that'd undo me.

II.

She was only six when she lost
her father. He bestowed on her
a name so large
it took twenty-one strokes to complete.

It's as if the love he had
was so great, the absence
hollows her continuously—
her longing, a love she could've known,
grew a vacant meteor in her
that could not collide with a planet
but was doomed to ablate.[2]
Her mother and sisters turned jealous,

her brothers—but a false wish
of heirs who couldn't carry his name.
How long before father's grace
again? Looking at her husband now,

thoughts of men weigh on her crown
'til pain has nowhere else
to bolt but out of her mouth.
She sits atop her father's throne—

no one shall be a man before her.

III.

I stood many times, blushes
bursting my cheeks—
the ticket agents, the grocers,
the butchers of every kind, butchered.
I imagined their spilled blood
coursing through me,
trafficking my veins,
tempering me.
I learn her words' icy brink,
sharpen blade on whetstones,
that pure speak of my line—

my mother's tongue
harbored by the no-poker-face stock
like the Szechuan-chili dragon-spit
that burns through the iron skillet.
Rootless as we are
even with a wish to leave,
we couldn't—we can't.
A well of bones, an ocean harboring fire—
I slash the water every day
with my sword,
divide my reflection in half
endlessly, trying to cut
a son out of a woman's gaze.

---

[2] "Meteor ablation occurs when a meteor travels through the Earth's atmosphere and the aerodynamic pressure of the surrounding atmosphere surpasses the material strength of the object." Mehta, Chris et al. "Caveats to Exogenous Organic Delivery from Ablation, Dilution, and Thermal Degradation." *Life (Basel)*. Jun. 8, 2018.

Expired *LA Times* Subscription

And all the news just repeats itself / Like some forgotten dream that we've both seen

— John Prine, "Hello in There"

When the sales rep asks if you'd like to renew
your subscription, you reply, "oh dear, I don't plan on
living another year," then you hang up.

I imagine the stunned rep holding the receiver,
venting to her colleague.
But your infamy doesn't spread.

You get the phone call again
from another rep in 2 months.
This is my favorite story about you. I tell it

during happy hour because it makes death
sound like a sassy girl friend who barges in
and insists, "grrrl, put on your best outfit

because we're going somewhere *special* tonight,"
and won't take no for an answer.
How many times exactly did you say no?

For a long time, I blamed the *Times*
because I thought only if it had been more
persistent about convincing you to extend

the subscription, you wouldn't have left.
You would still be at your home
because you couldn't get over your curiosity

of what new assholery the paper
would deliver to your door the next day.
Today, I ask a salesperson on the phone,

*Why does the news keep repeating
when fewer ears are alive to hear?*
But on the disconnected line, no answer.

Do Not Ask Why

I am but a fever of stingrays,
rising terribly toward the drowned sky.

Archeology of a Phone Call

3:00 PM

When I pick up the phone, my mother is breathless,
in the middle of a conversation we didn't have.
She told me that she is a Buddha incarnate.
Her sister has a sort of Chinese
that you can't just wring out of your mug.
Mental illness runs in the family, you know,
but on my mom's side. I was spared
because I was my father's favorite.

3:30 PM

Her little brother, her only younger sibling,
moved their parents' grave
to the flood zone, and every night since
her parents floated down to her in dreams,
waking her with the cold drips from their hair.
She once thought about drinking enough bleach
till she was pure and faultless.
She didn't go through with it, she says,
but she did throw up for two days.

4:00 PM

She plants in me her dad, who died early,
so she spent the rest of her life autopsying him.
His fever, his voice, and his fear of heights she kept,
but the last memory of his alcohol breath
she let her siblings ransack among the remains.
She says she sees herself in my eyes.
I watch her as she uses scissors
on her skin to cut out the tongue
inside her veins that won't stop screaming.

5:00 PM

See how the world looked
like a stadium of adoring lit BIC lighters
from that six-hundred-foot balcony—
they say vertigo is just another way of loving
death. Had I not wished for such love
as I pulled her in from the ledge?
There are thorny wails threaded
through our voices. We seem to keep
talking over each other, overcoming
one another, like we know
between us there is a chasm.

5:05 PM

I forget to respond to her last remark.
There's a brief static in the phone.
Her silence sizzles against my skin.
I gather her father's syllables from the floor
to ask what else her sister did.
She's a crazy bitch, you know.
We share a laugh.
Like normal people.
Her voice flowers in my phone again.

What Jesus Said While in Line for the Bathroom

Shit is a more onerous theological problem than is evil . . . [because] [t]he responsibility for shit . . . rests entirely with Him, the creator of man.

— Milan Kundera, *The Unbearable Lightness of Being*

It's a shame that an absent father
figure should define me so much
when I am still a son to a mother.

When the breezes pierce with the matchmakers'
tattles, I get tired of being the anointed one,
written on the nails by suffering beholders,

shaped into a figurine or a painting
that shows how I bleed and bleed
even as my abs get better over time.

I don't have any blood left in my veins
but boredom from hanging everywhere.
I am more than the sad eyes that follow

while you exit past the pews
after a long-winded sermon about whores.
I never wanted to be a poster child

for the celibate because I am
also a minister of the flesh.
I did not intend to disguise shit.

The bathroom stall without a lock—
this is a matter of wine
and salt. Desire is the dirty miracle

that lets me walk on the Sea of Galilee.
So, dearest, take me by my waist,
and swear me by my given name—

Jesus H. Christ.

Firstborn

When I was young, my mother threw a boiling pot
at me, and I burnt all night wrapped in a blanket
of soup and cabbage until only dried stains
remained in the daylight. But I kept healing.
So she threw more: plates, knives dulled
gray with dishwater until she knew I was born
with a heart ravenous for grief. She hurled down more—
wishing stones that never skipped across water,
each one shrilling a metallic clang and then gone.

Since life first forced its breath into my virgin
lungs, my mother fights against her own end, spins
thirteen monster-stepmothers betrothed to her ghost-
riddled husband. They keep burying the kids in the dirt,
and, even resting her eyes, they're all mother sees.

And I, love, I am the improbability, the municipal
hunger, the continental evil, the famed firstborn—
how my living warms and pains her.

Humming and Shaving

To really shave above the knee for the satisfaction that may not even be mine, I writhe and twist myself into the meanest of positions. There's no yoga pose for turn-your-head-till-you-overcome-double-vision-to-spot-the-straggler-pubic-hair. I'm dizzy. But this may be from the glass of wine I drank before because I couldn't get started without one. I hum a song about Judgment Day—the humdrum must glisten. I wonder if a monogamous woman shaves the way I do for one man. How could she not have placed so much hope in him? If I shaved once, I've shaved for a century. Always up, not down. Bending where the hair grows. The danger of nicks from the uncertain grip lurking along every sinew, a road I can never master because my testicles never rest the same. Existence is a pouch held together by others' gaze. What would the Seventies feminists think of me? No, I was not born ready. I cut and buff and spackle myself into a version of a human. My cleanliness impersonates innocence. The drops I wipe off trill as a lark. With all that effort, I cannot wait around for a muse to find me. I will find him, with the care of a has-been lamb who never wanted to be a lamb. And when I do, I will commit my favorite parts of him to paper, kiss the smart smack out of his mouth—render him more beautiful than hell is right.

A Hole in the Sky

I once saw something I can't explain.

I saw my grandfather looking
through the window of my second-story apartment,

his bald eyes peeling
back my sins,
especially the ones I enjoyed.

Locked in an eternal staring contest with him,
I forgot I'd been awake for two days
until I twitched. Surrounded by the blistering, chill air

where god and devil meet, he melted
into the pane's hollow imprint
of the moon.

The next morning, I inspected the building,
but found no anchoring bricks large enough
to provide a step up to my window.

I was sad to see the remains I had of him explained
by the lack of grimy footprints—

I thought he had clawed back into the world
that erased him to hand me
a twenty-dollar bill

he always sent me on my birthday—
the only way he knew how to communicate
when he was near the end.

On nights when sleep can't erase me,
I listen to a moon as blank as him

as it talks of things he never could.

You Will Be Done[3]

Even though I asked her not to bring gifts,
my mother's luggage spits out dreams—
decoys, owls, and jeweled elephants—
loot she plucked out from lands she knows

only by tales. I ask if she'd like to travel more.
An ocean is an ocean is an ocean.
She unwraps the newspapers from the china she kept
for thirty years because she never had an occasion.

Over coffee, we indulge in our favorite pastime:
talking about other people's pain. Her sister,
the one who bullied her the most,
is dying; diabetes will claim her feet, but the rest

of her, the devil already took when she signed
away the house their mother was to retire in.
Mother shows pictures from her youth—
some of her cohorts, she's heard, have died too.

She wonders if her goodbye would've meant anything.
She moves on to the kitchen sink, starts scrubbing
the counters with rattling love. She mends
the vacuity of my home among the pots and pans.

I must have peddled my country to the enemy,
she says as she refuses to use a mop and crawls
the floor with a rag. In her past life, she was human.
She asks about a calendar she left here years ago.

We dump the old newspapers and walk around
as the sun sheds the last of today's weary miracles.
Out of gifts, out of time, out of masks,
she waits for her kingdom to come.

---

[3] This poet kept misreading "thy kingdom come, thy will be done" in his youth.

My Father's Mother That My Mother Hated

I loom languid over her in the hospital,
    as we quickly run out of things to say.

            Did they bring you a good meal?
                  Yes, my father's flight got delayed—

he'll be here as soon as he can.

That last one, we both know, is a lie.
        A product of you, her absent favorite son,
    and the woman whose scorn

            she underestimated—
                I hurt
more than comfort.

    Despite six children, they pointedly say,
she made sure she had her fun—

        she never stopped working at Shiseido,
    never stopped wearing their makeup,
            and stayed out with her mahjong circle.

Now next to her bed, I still hear the rumors:
                she hovered over her children
    rather than raised them.

My visits to the hospital get shorter,
        and my nights out alone at bars
            get longer. Many nights

I see the bartenders hula-hoop the night to a finale.

    My only motivation to wake up early
        is the McDonald's breakfast of spam and eggs.

I tell myself I want to reconnect with the land where I was born
                            and walk the way to the hospital,
    but when I show up in the afternoon

again but a messy silhouette of you,
        she doesn't need to say
                            it's too late for us.

                I thought I saw her gaze
    grapple far beyond the island.

Every day, I ask doctors questions
        about her condition, swirling
                the medical jargon around my mouth
                        until they harden in my crab-shell throat.

I just want every man to tell me all the truth.

    The messy,
        meandering clamor,

where words like *lesions*
                and *interventional*
    are thrown about,

comes down to a decision;
    a decision that is not mine

to make
    is made—
            to cut her open for the last time.

In the postoperative bed, she is unconscious,

    yet I hear her cries hurling themselves
        to the window every time I look in.

Her breath phantoms fog in her mask,
            laps up to the glass divider like a hundred waves,

    each with a mouth that could hold a universe of hurt.

A hellish choir,
              erasing the parts of me that do not resemble you.

Shortly after you arrive at the hospital and rush to her side,

      the fog clears
               and the song stops.

No man ever thought to tell me
                she knew exactly when to leave.

In the Thick Night, We Kiss the Flame

Everyone has gone to bed, except I keep going out for a cigarette. I see the hotel clerk smoking, too. Back at his desk, he talks about his life, reveals his plastic leg. I wish we were sharing a pale whiskey drink and spilling it in between laughs. This is not a boisterous laugh, but one that bandages over wounds; the accident that took his leg—*clean off*, he says. But everything that followed is messy. This laugh is a kind of crime we use to blindside tragedy when it takes so much from us. He can't hold rifles anymore either, he says. The accident happened overseas when he was transporting his army buddies to safety. He doesn't mention the attackers. We go for another cigarette. The doctor told him there's a chance his body will reject the plastic. A very high chance. In the middle of us all is a cigarette butt whose flame refuses to die. Despite the repeated stepping out, its smoke rises. Our conversation turns god-ward. Neither of us believe, but we like the word *miracle*. He asks if I know any jokes that he can tell his eleven-year-old niece—I tell the dirtiest joke I know just to be a prick. His laughter is a blood cry. Then suddenly, as if I were a mother, I pray for the health of a heathen son—pray for him to find a good woman. But I keep that thought to myself as he talks about how he ended up in prison.

I follow to the edge of his story, to the edge of laughter.

About the Author

Jeremy Ra is a queer, Chinese-Korean-American poet living in Los Angeles. A Pushcart nominee, his poems have appeared or will appear in *I-70 Review*, *Cultural Daily*, *San Diego Poetry Annual*, and *Catamaran Literary Reader*, among others. He was the recipient of the 2022 Morton Marcus Poetry Prize and a finalist for the Steve Kowit Poetry Prize.

Acknowledgements

Thank you to the editors of the following publications where some of these poems and their earlier versions have first appeared:

A Journal of Radical Wonder	"Do Not Ask Why," "You Will Be Done"
A Moon of One's Own	"A Hole in the Sky" – Best of the Net nominee
Catamaran Literary Reader	"Dumplings (*Jiao Zi*)" – Winner of 2022 Morton Marcus Poetry Prize
Cultural Daily	"What Jesus Said While in Line for the Bathroom – Pushcart Nominee
Glimpse	"The Audition"
I-70 Review	"Humanity," "Last Time I Saw Eve"

My sincere thank you to Suzanne Lummis, Alexis Rhone Fancher, Ron Koertge, Aruni Wijesinghe, Mei Xian Qiu, Katie McArthy, and Eric Morago for their support, mentorship, and encouragement - without them, this book would not have been possible. Further, thank you to all my beloved, estimable instructors and fellow poets from Catamaran Conference, Napa Valley Conference, Deep Poetry Knowledge, The Write After, STRATA Master Class, Kim's Sunday Afternoon Workshop, and Your Poem, Your Voice Workshop. And thank you to all my friends and family, who fill me to the brim with the lust to tell.

Also Available from Moon Tide Press

Kissing the Wound, J.D. Isip (2023)
Feed It to the River, Terhi K. Cherry (2022)
Beat Not Beat: An Anthology of California Poets Screwing on the Beat and Post-Beat Tradition (2022)
When There Are Nine: Poems Celebrating the Life and Achievements of Ruth Bader Ginsburg (2022)
The Knife Thrower's Daughter, Terri Niccum (2022)
2 Revere Place, Aruni Wijesinghe (2022)
Here Go the Knives, Kelsey Bryan-Zwick (2022)
Trumpets in the Sky, Jerry Garcia (2022)
Threnody, Donna Hilbert (2022)
A Burning Lake of Paper Suns, Ellen Webre (2021)
Instructions for an Animal Body, Kelly Gray (2021)
Head *V* Heart: New & Selected Poems, Rob Sturma (2021)
Sh!t Men Say to Me: A Poetry Anthology in Response to Toxic Masculinity (2021)
Flower Grand First, Gustavo Hernandez (2021)
Everything is Radiant Between the Hates, Rich Ferguson (2020)
When the Pain Starts: Poetry as Sequential Art, Alan Passman (2020)
This Place Could Be Haunted If I Didn't Believe in Love, Lincoln McElwee (2020)
Impossible Thirst, Kathryn de Lancellotti (2020)
Lullabies for End Times, Jennifer Bradpiece (2020)
Crabgrass World, Robin Axworthy (2020)
Contortionist Tongue, Dania Ayah Alkhouli (2020)
The only thing that makes sense is to grow, Scott Ferry (2020)
Dead Letter Box, Terri Niccum (2019)
Tea and Subtitles: Selected Poems 1999-2019, Michael Miller (2019)
At the Table of the Unknown, Alexandra Umlas (2019)
The Book of Rabbits, Vince Trimboli (2019)
Everything I Write Is a Love Song to the World, David McIntire (2019)
Letters to the Leader, HanaLena Fennel (2019)
Darwin's Garden, Lee Rossi (2019)
Dark Ink: A Poetry Anthology Inspired by Horror (2018)
Drop and Dazzle, Peggy Dobreer (2018)
Junkie Wife, Alexis Rhone Fancher (2018)
The Moon, My Lover, My Mother, & the Dog, Daniel McGinn (2018)
Lullaby of Teeth: An Anthology of Southern California Poetry (2017)
Angels in Seven, Michael Miller (2016)
A Likely Story, Robbi Nester (2014)

Embers on the Stairs, Ruth Bavetta (2014)
The Green of Sunset, John Brantingham (2013)
The Savagery of Bone, Timothy Matthew Perez (2013)
The Silence of Doorways, Sharon Venezio (2013)
Cosmos: An Anthology of Southern California Poetry (2012)
Straws and Shadows, Irena Praitis (2012)
In the Lake of Your Bones, Peggy Dobreer (2012)
I Was Building Up to Something, Susan Davis (2011)
Hopeless Cases, Michael Kramer (2011)
One World, Gail Newman (2011)
What We Ache For, Eric Morago (2010)
Now and Then, Lee Mallory (2009)
Pop Art: An Anthology of Southern California Poetry (2009)
In the Heaven of Never Before, Carine Topal (2008)
A Wild Region, Kate Buckley (2008)
Carving in Bone: An Anthology of Orange County Poetry (2007)
Kindness from a Dark God, Ben Trigg (2007)
A Thin Strand of Lights, Ricki Mandeville (2006)
Sleepyhead Assassins, Mindy Nettifee (2006)
Tide Pools: An Anthology of Orange County Poetry (2006)
Lost American Nights: Lyrics & Poems, Michael Ubaldini (2006)

Patrons

Moon Tide Press would like to thank the following people for their support in helping publish the finest poetry from the Southern California region. To sign up as a patron, visit www.moontidepress.com or send an email to publisher@moontidepress.com.

Anonymous
Robin Axworthy
Conner Brenner
Nicole Connolly
Bill Cushing
Susan Davis
Kristen Baum DeBeasi
Peggy Dobreer
Kate Gale
Dennis Gowans
Alexis Rhone Fancher
HanaLena Fennel
Half Off Books & Brad T. Cox
Donna Hilbert
Jim & Vicky Hoggatt
Michael Kramer
Ron Koertge & Bianca Richards
Gary Jacobelly
Ray & Christi Lacoste
Jeffery Lewis
Zachary & Tammy Locklin
Lincoln McElwee
David McIntire
José Enrique Medina
Michael Miller & Rachanee Srisavasdi
Michelle & Robert Miller
Ronny & Richard Morago
Terri Niccum
Andrew November
Jeremy Ra
Luke & Mia Salazar
Jennifer Smith
Roger Sponder
Andrew Turner
Rex Wilder
Mariano Zaro
Wes Bryan Zwick

www.ingramcontent.com/pod-product-compliance
Lightning Source LLC
Chambersburg PA
CBHW021001090426
42736CB00010B/1418